NOVELLO
classics
for the flute

C. Debussy

Syrinx

or La Flûte de Pan

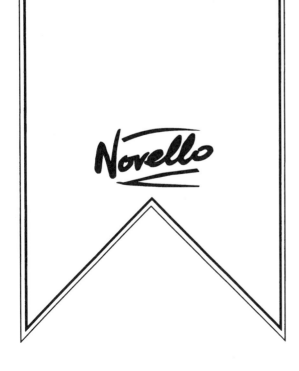

Novello Publishing Limited

Order No. NOV 120756

La Flûte de Pan
or
Syrinx

PSYCHE, Act III, Scene One.

Pan's cave. Through the opening you can see a clearing in the forest. A stream flows into a little lake. White rocks in the background. In the moonlight, nymphs in white are dancing; other nymphs pick flowers or lie by the water's edge. At times they all stop to listen in wonder to the syrinx of the invisible Pan.

CLAUDE DEBUSSY

L'Oréade:
Listen to Pan beginning to play his flute again.

La Naiade:
It's as if night had un-buckled its belt and let the stars fall onto the silent earth, twinkling melodiously. Surely Eurydice's lover couldn't have made such sublime and moving sounds on his lyre?

L'Oréade:
Keep silent, contain your joy, listen.

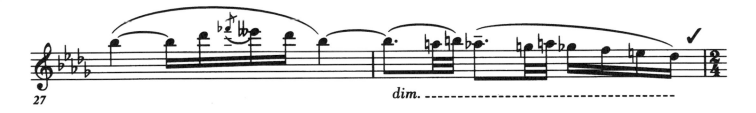

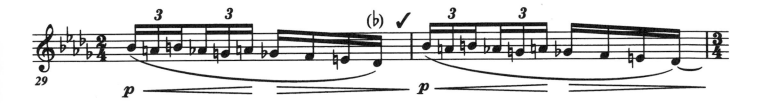

La Flûte de Pan was written at the request of the playwright Gabriel Mourey as incidental music to his play *Psyché*, and was first performed in Paris on 1 December 1913. Mourey asked Debussy to write 'the last melody that Pan plays before his death'. On receiving a copy of the lines during which the music was to be performed, Debussy directed that it be played out of sight in the wings of the stage.

Louis Fleury, the dedicatee, gave the première, subsequently often performing it on his concert tours. Fleury was said to have insisted that a screen always be provided behind which he would play *La Flûte de Pan*.

As the music was written to be played simultaneously with La Naïade's lines, the directions for the stage setting and the introductory and incidental lines are reproduced here as an indica-tion of the background.

Although *La Flûte de Pan* was well enough known to French flutists, Louis Fleury owned the only copy of the score, and the work remained unpublished until after his death in 1926. According to Marcel Moyse, the publisher Jobert obtained the manuscript from Mme Fleury and asked Moyse to prepare it for publication. Moyse added some breathing marks and possibly added a slur or two where there were inconsistencies in the manuscript. It was published in 1927 for the first time under its subtitle, *Syrinx*.

Though this short masterpiece reflects the delightful lines of Mourey, it is also a lament, for Pan will play no more; through his syrinx, he sensuously looks back upon his former conquests and his love of beautiful nymphs.

Performing Notes

The Jobert autograph is probably lost, but an autographed copy[1] now in Brussels brings to light some important differences between it and the Jobert Edition of *Syrinx*. This edition is based on the Brussels autograph.

In the Brussels autograph, there are only three commas which may indicate breathing or phrases: the end of bar 2 and the middle of bars 4 and 14. The other breathing indications are the usual ones except that the traditional breath at the end of bar 16 – in the middle of the second subject – reflects Moyse's own breathing problems since childhood, as described in the editor's biography of him[2]. The breath in bar 25 was suggested by Moyse: 'I remember Debussy asking me *not* to breathe here, but I couldn't do it.' Moyse told Debussy 'for me it is not possible'. This breath should therefore be avoided if possible. The breaths at the end of bars 28 and 29 were preferred by the composer ac-cording to Moyse. A breath appears after the first beat of bar 31 in Jobert but should be avoided in order to make a longer phrase. Neither the *diminuendo* in bar 31, nor the *subito piano* at the beginning of bars 15 and 17 appears in Jobert, but they do in the Brussels autograph.

The accent on the first beat of the penultimate bar has always been doubtful. When the editor asked Moyse about this is 1968, he said he thought it was a mistake and should have been a *diminuendo*. The Brussels autograph proves his point. This accent which has puzzled flutists the world over can now be omitted.

An important performing point: Debussy's orchestral and piano works make frequent use of —————— *p* which is, in effect, *subito piano*. Although not written as *subito*, this is implied and should be performed as such.

Trevor Wye, 1994

The following story was found in Marcel Moyse's personal notebook[3] and must surely depict the mythological tale as Moyse and other flutists understood it:

'Syrinx, you must know, was of old not an instrument, but a beautiful maiden, with a melodious voice. She fed her goats, sported with the Nymphs, and sang as the now [sic] does. As she was thus pasturing, sporting and singing, Pan approached her and sought to persuade her to yield to his desires, promising that all her she-goats would bear twins at a birth. The girl mocked at his suit, saying she would never accept a lover who was neither goat nor wholly human. Pan darted after her to take her perforce, and Syrinx fled Pan and his violence. When she was wearied in her flight, she hid in some reeds and so disappeared in a marsh. In his rage Pan slashed down the reeds, and when he could not find the girl and perceived what had happened, he contrived this instrument. The reeds which he bound with wax he made unequal, because their love had been unequal. And so, she who was once a beautiful maiden is now a musical pipe.'

1) A facsimile of the Autograph with notes, and part of the text of the play, is published by Autographus Musiscus, Malmö, Sweden, with an introduction by Anders Ljungar-Chapelon.
2) See 'The Story of Syrinx', p.67 in *Marcel Moyse, An Extraordinary Man*. Trevor Wye, Winzer Press, U.S.A., 1993.
3) Now in the editor's possession. The extract is in English in the original.

La flûte de Pan ou Syrinx

La flûte de Pan, composée à la demande du dramaturge Gabriel Mourey comme musique de scène pour sa pièce *Psyché*, fut créée à Paris le 1er décembre 1913. Mourey demanda à Debussy d'imaginer "la dernière mélodie que joue Pan avant de mourir". Après avoir pris connaissance des vers sur lesquels serait jouée sa musique, Debussy souhaita que celle-ci soit exécutée hors de la scène, depuis les coulisses.

Louis Fleury créa l'oeuvre, dont il était le dédicataire, et la donna souvent par la suite lors de ses tournées de concerts. Il aurait toujours insisté pour jouer *La flûte de Pan* derrière un écran.

Cette pièce ayant été écrite pour être jouée simultanément à la déclamation des vers de la Naïade, les indications scéniques, les vers d'introduction et le poème sont reproduits ici en illustration de ce contexte.

La flûte de Pan était parfaitement connue des flûtistes français mais Louis Fleury possédait l'unique exemplaire de la partition. L'oeuvre ne fut publiée qu'après sa mort en 1926. Selon Marcel Moyse, l'éditeur Jobert obtint le manuscrit de Madame Fleury et chargea Moyse de sa préparation en vue de son édition. Moyse y ajouta certaines indications de respiration et peut-être une ou deux liaisons là où le manuscrit présentait quelques confusions. L'oeuvre parut pour la première fois en 1932 sous son sous-titre de *Syrinx*.

Tout en reflétant les vers délicats de Mourey, ce chef-d'oeuvre de concision illustre la lamentation de Pan qui ne jouera plus. A travers sa syrinx, il se souvient avec volupté de ses anciennes conquêtes et de son amour pour les belles nymphes.

Observations sur l'exécution

L'autographe parvenu à Jobert est probablement perdu et un copie authentifiée[1], conservée à Bruxelles, présente un certain nombre de différence importantes avec l'édition Jobert de *Syrinx*. Notre édition repose sur l'autographe de Bruxelles.

Dans ce dernier ne figurent que trois virgules pouvant être des indications de respiration ou de phrases: à la fin de la mesure 2 et au milieu des mesures 4 et 14. Les autres indications de respirations sont celles habituellement admises, à l'exception de celle usuelle, de la fin de la mesure 16 – au milieu du deuxième thème – liée, d'après la biographie du musicien établie par son éditeur[2], aux problèmes respiratoires que Moyse avait depuis l'enfance. La coupure de la mesure 25 fut suggérée par Moyse qui rappela: "Debussy me demanda de *ne pas* respirer à cet endroit, mais j'en étais incapable." Moyse répliqua ainsi à Debussy: "Pour moi c'est impossible". On évitera donc, si possible, cette respiration. Debussy préférait, toujours d'après Moyse, que l'on respire à la fin des mesures 28 et 29. On écartera la respiration qui intervient après le premier temps de la mesure 31 de l'édition Jobert pour constituer une phrase plus longue. Ni le *diminuendo* de la mesure 31, ni le *subito piano* du début des mesures 15 et 17, apparaissant dans l'autographe de Bruxelles, ne figurent dans l'édition Jobert.

L'accent placé sur le premier temps de l'avant-dernière mesure a toujours été discutable. Moyse, à qui son éditeur soumit la question en 1968, s'affirma convaincu qu'il s'agissait d'une erreur qui aurait dû être corrigée par un *diminuendo*. L'autographe de Bruxelles confirme cet avis. On peut donc supprimer cette accentuation qui a perturbé les flûtistes du monde entier.

Mentionnons ici un autre élément important concernant l'exécution: les oeuvres pour orchestre et pour piano de Debussy ont souvent recours au signe ⎯⎯⎯ *p* qui, en réalité est un *piano subito*. Bien que le terme *subito* n'apparaisse pas, il est sous-entendu et il faut en tenir compte dans l'interprétation.

Trevor Wye, 1994

Cet extrait du carnet de notes personnel de Marcel Moyse[3] exprime la façon dont les flûtistes ont abordé ce conte mythologique:

"Syrinx, vous savez, n'était pas anciennement un instrument de musique mais une belle jeune fille à la voix mélodieuse. Elle gardait ses chèvres, badinait avec les nymphes et chantait. Alors qu'elle badinait et chantait ainsi en gardant ses chèvres, Pan s'approcha d'elle et tenta de la persuader d'accéder à ses désirs, lui promettant que toutes ses chèvres mettraient bas deux chevreaux. La jeune fille se rit de son accoutrement et lui dit qu'elle n'accepterait jamais un amant qui ne soit ni homme ni chèvre. Pan la poursuivit pour la prendre de force mais Syrinx échappa à sa violence. Epuisée par sa course, elle se cacha dans les roseaux et disparut dans le marais. Dans sa colère, Pan tailla les roseaux. Ne retrouvant pas la jeune fille, il comprit ce qui s'était passé et inventa son instrument de musique. Les roseaux qu'il lia avec de la cire étaient de longueurs inégales, à l'image de l'inégalité de leur amour. C'est ainsi que cette belle jeune fille donna son nom à une flûte."

1) Un *fac-simile* de l'autographe, accompagné de commentaires, d'une partie du texte de la pièce et précédé d'une introduction d'Anders Ljungar-Chapelon, est édité chez Autographus Musiscus, Malmö (Suède).
2) Voir "The Story of Syrinx" dans: Trevor Wye, *Marcel Moyse, an Extraordinary Man*, 1993, Winzer Press (USA), p.67
3) Actuellement en possession de l'éditeur. Cet extrait est rédigé à l'origine en langue anglaise.

Psyché, Acte III, Scène 1

La scène représente la grotte de Pan; par sa large ouverture, on aperçoit une clairière au cœur de la forêt touffue. Dans la prairie, un ruisseau passe, formant un petit lac. Rochers blancs au fond . . . Dans la clairière, des nymphes dansent, vont et viennent, toutes vêtues de blanc, avec des poses harmonieuses. D'autres cueillent des fleurs, d'autres, étendues au bord de l'eau, s'y mirent. Par moments elles s'arrêtent toutes, émerveillées, écoutant la syrinx de Pan invisible, émues par le chant qui s'échappe des roseaux creux.

L'Oréade: . . . Mais voici que Pan de sa flûte recommence a jouer . . .
La Naïade: . . . Prodige! Il semble que la Nuit ait dénoué sa ceinture et qu'en écartant ses voiles elle ait laissé, pour se jouer, sur la terre tomber toutes les étoiles . . . Crois-tu que l'amant d'Eurydice faisait vibrer de plus touchants et plus sublimes chants les cordes d'airain de sa lyre? Non, n'est-ce pas?
L'Oréade: Tais-toi, contiens ta joie, écoute.

La Flûte de Pan oder Syrinx

La Flûte de Pan entstand auf Wunsch des Dramatikers Gabriel Mourey als Bühnenmusik zu seinem Theaterstück *Psyché* und wurde erstmals am 1. Dezember 1913 in Paris aufgeführt. Mourey bat Debussy, 'die letzte Melodie, die Pan spielt, bevor er stirbt' zu schreiben. Als Debussy eine Kopie jener Zeilen erhielt, während denen die Musik gespielt werden sollte, bestimmte er, daß sie außer Sichtweite, in den Flügeln des Theaters ausgeführt werden sollte.

Louis Fleury, dem das Stück gewidmet war, spielte es während der Premiere und führte es später häufig auf seinen Konzerttourneen auf. Fleury soll darauf bestanden haben, daß es immer eine Trennwand gab, hinter der er *La Flûte de Pan* spielte.

Da die Musik gleichzeitig mit La Naïades Zeilen erklingen sollte, geben wir hier die Bühnenanweisungen und die einleitenden und begleitenden Zeilen wieder, um auf den Hintergrund zu verweisen.

Obwohl *La Flûte de Pan* französischen Flötisten durchaus bekannt war, besaß Louis Fleury die einzige Kopie der Partitur, und das Werk wurde erst nach seinem Tod 1926 veröffentlicht. Laut Marcel Moyse erhielt der Verleger Jobert das Manuskript von Mme Fleury und bat Moyse, es für die Veröffentlichung vorzubereiten. Moyse fügte einige Atmungszeichen und möglicherweise ein oder zwei Bindungen hinzu, wo es im Manuskript Widersprüche gab. Das Manuskript wurde 1927 erstmals unter seinem Untertitel *Syrinx* veröffentlicht.

Obwohl dieses kurze Meisterwerk die wunderbaren Zeilen von Mourey spiegelt, ist es auch eine Klage, denn Pan wird nicht mehr musizieren; durch seine Syrinx blickt er sinnlich zurück auf seine früheren Eroberungen und seine Liebe zu schönen Nymphen.

Hinweise zur Aufführung

Das Jobert-Autograph ist wahrscheinlich verschollen, eine autographe Kopie[1], die sich jetzt in Brüssel befindet, bringt jedoch einige bedeutende Unterschiede zwischen ihm und der Jobert-Ausgabe von *Syrinx* ans Licht. Die vorliegende Ausgabe beruht auf dem Brüsseler Autograph.

Im Brüsseler Autograph finden sich nur drei Kommas, die möglicherweise auf Atempausen oder Phrasen hinweisen: das Ende von Takt 2 und die Mitte von Takten 4 und 14. Die anderen Atemhinweise sind die üblichen, abgesehen davon, daß die herkömmliche Pause am Ende von Takt 16 – in der Mitte des zweiten Themas – Moyses Atemprobleme, die aus seiner Kindheit stammen und vom Herausgeber in Moyses Biographie beschrieben werden, widerspiegelt[2]. Die Pause in Takt 25 wurde von Moyse vorgeschlagen: 'Ich erinnere mich, daß Debussy mich bat, hier *nicht* zu atmen, aber es ging einfach nicht.' Er teilte Debussy mit 'es ist mir nicht möglich'. Diese Pause sollte daher möglichst vermieden werden. Die Pausen am Ende von den Takten 28 und 29 zog der Komponist laut Moyse vor. Nach dem ersten Schlag in Takt 31 erscheint bei Jobert eine Atempause; sie sollte jedoch vermieden werden, um eine längere Phrase zu erhalten. Weder das *diminuendo* in Takt 31 noch das *subito piano* zu Beginn von Takten 15 und 17, die beide im Brüsseler Autograph vorkommen, erscheinen bei Jobert.

Die Betonung auf dem ersten Schlag des vorletzten Taktes war immer etwas zweifelhaft. Als der Herausgeber Moyse 1968 danach fragte, meinte er, daß es sich wohl um einen Fehler handelt und ein *diminuendo* sein sollte. Das Brüsseler Autograph bestätigt dies. Dieser Akzent, der Flötisten auf der ganzen Welt verwirrt hat, kann nun weggelassen werden.

Ein wichtiger Aufführungspunkt: Debussys orchestrale Kompositionen und Klavierwerke verwenden häufig ⏵ *p*, bei dem es sich um *subito piano* handelt. Obwohl nicht *subito* geschrieben wird, ist dies doch stillschweigend inbegriffen und sollte als solches gespielt werden.

Trevor Wye, 1994

Die folgende Geschichte fand sich in Marcel Moyses persönlichem Notizbuch[3] und schildert die mythologische Geschichte, wie Moyse und andere Flötisten sie verstanden:

'Syrinx, das muß man wissen, war zunächst kein Instrument, sondern eine wunderschöne Jungfrau mit melodischer Stimme. Sie fütterte ihre Ziegen, spielte mit den Nymphen und sang so wie jetzt. Als sie so am Weiden, Spielen und Singen war, trat Pan zu ihr und versuchte, sie zu überreden, sich seinem Verlangen hinzugeben. Er versprach ihr, daß all ihre Ziegen Zwillinge gebären würden. Das Mädchen machte sich über sein Werben lustig und sagte, es würde nie einen Geliebten annehmen, der weder Ziege noch ganz Mensch war. Pan lief ihr nach, um sie gewaltsam zu nehmen, und Syrinx floh vor Pan und seiner Gewalt. Als sie auf der Flucht ermüdete, versteckte sie sich im Schilf und verschwand so in einem Sumpf. In seiner Wut mähte Pan das Schilf nieder, und als er das Mädchen nicht finden konnte und feststellte, was passiert war, erfand er dieses Instrument. Das Schilfrohr, das er mit Wachs zusammenband, ließ er unterschiedlich lang, da auch ihre Liebe unterschiedlich gewesen war. Und so ist sie, die einst ein schöne Jungfrau war, nun eine musikalische Flöte.'

1) Ein Faksimile des Autographs mit Anmerkungen und Teilen des Schauspieltextes ist von Autographus Musiscus, Malmö, Schweden, mit einer Einleitung von Anders Ljungar-Chapelon veröffentlicht worden.
2) Vgl. 'The Story of Syrinx' ('Die Geschichte von Syrinx'), S. 67 in *Marcel Moyse, An Extraordinary Man*. Trevor Wye, Winzer Press, U.S.A., 1993.
3) Jetzt im Besitz des Herausgebers. Der Auszug steht im Original in Englisch.

Psyché, Akt III, Erste Szene

Pans Höhle. Durch die Öffnung kann man eine Lichtung im Wald sehen. Ein Bach fließt in einen kleinen See. Weiße Felsen im Hintergrund. Im Mondschein tanzen weißgekleidete Nymphen; andere Nymphen pflücken Blumen oder liegen am Wasserrand. Manchmal halten sie alle inne und hören erstaunt der Syrinx des unsichtbaren Pan zu.

L'Oréade: Hör zu, wie Pan wieder anfängt, Flöte zu spielen.
La Naïade: Es ist, als ob die Nacht ihren Gürtel geöffnet hat und die Sterne auf die stille Erde fallen und melodisch funkeln ließ. Sicher hätte Euridices Geliebter nicht so erhabene und bewegende Töne auf seiner Leier erzeugen können?
L'Oréade: Sei still, zügle Deine Freude, hör zu.

La Flûte de Pan o Syrinx

Il Flauto di Pan fu scritto, su richiesta del commediografo Gabriel Mourey, come musica di scena per la sua commedia *Psyché*, e la prima fu data a Parigi il 1 dicembre 1913. Mourey chiese a Debussy di scrivere 'l'ultima melodia che Pan suona prima della sua morte'. Ricevendo la copia dei versi che la musica doveva accompagnare, Debussy diede istruzioni che essa fosse eseguita fuori scena nelle quinte del palcoscenico.

Louis Fleury, il dedicatario ne fece la prima esecuzione e successivamente lo suonò spesso nelle sue tournée. Si dice che Fleury abbia sempre insistito per avere un siparietto dietro al quale suonare *Il Flauto di Pan*.

Poichè la musica fu scritta per essere suonata contemporaneamente ai versi de La Naïade, si sono riprodotti, per fornire un'idea del contesto, sia le istruzioni per la disposizione del palcoscenico sia i versi introduttivi e quelli incidentali.

Sebbene *Il Flauto di Pan* fosse ben conosciuto tra i flautisti francesi, Louis Fleury possedeva l'unica copia della partitura, e il lavoro rimase inedito fino a dopo la sua morte nel 1926. Secondo Marcel Moyse, l'editore Jobert ottenne il manoscritto dalla Signora Fleury e chiese a Moyse di prepararlo per la pubblicazione. Moyse aggiunse alcune indicazione di respiro e forse alcune legature dove c'erano delle incongruenze nella partitura. Fu pubblicato nel 1927 per la prima volta con il suo sottotitolo, *Syrinx*.

Sebbene questo breve capolavoro rifletta i deliziosi versi di Mourey, esso è anche un lamento dato che Pan non suonerà più successivamente; attraverso il suo syrinx, egli sensuosamente guarda indietro alle sue passate conquiste e al suo amore per le belle ninfe.

Note per l'esecuzione

Il manoscritto autografo di Jobert è probabilmente perduto, ma una copia autografa[1] correntemente a Bruxelles mette in luce alcune importanti differenze con l'edizione di *Syrinx* di Jobert. La nostra edizione si basa sull'autografo di Bruxelles.

Nell'autografo di Bruxelles ci sono soltanto tre segni di respiro o fraseggio: alla fine della battuta 2 e a metà delle battute 4 e 14. Gli altri respiri sono quelli convezionali fatta eccezione per quello tradizionale alla fine di battuta 16 – nel mezzo del secondo soggetto – che è dovuto a un personale problema di respirazione di Moyse, contratto nella fanciullezza, come descritto nella sua biografia[2] a cura del revisore. Il respiro a battuta 25 fu suggerito da Moyse: 'Ricordo che Debussy mi chiese di *non* respirare in questo punto, ma purtroppo non potevo evitarlo'. Moyse disse a Debussy 'per me non è possibile'. Questo respiro deve di conseguenza essere evitato, se possibile. Secondo Moyse i respiri alla fine delle battute 28 e 29 erano preferiti da Debussy. Un respiro compare dopo il primo movimento della battuta 31 nell'edizione di Jobert, ma deve essere possibilmente evitato per ottenere una frase più lunga. Nè il diminuendo a battuta 31, nè il subito piano all'inizio di battuta 15 e 17 compaiono nella Jobert, ma entrambi appaiono nell'autografo di Bruxelles.

L'accento sul primo movimento della penultima battuta è sempre stato dubbio. Quando il revisore interpellò Moyse in proposito nel 1968, egli rispose che pensava fosse un errore e avrebbe dovuto essere un diminuendo. L'autografo di Bruxelles conferma questo punto di vista. Questo accento che ha reso perplessi flautisti di tutto il mondo può essere ora abolito.

Un osservazione importante per l'esecuzione: I lavori orchestrali e pianistici di Debussy fanno uso frequente di ◁▭▭ *p*, che è in effetti un subito piano. Anche se il subito è omesso, rimane sottinteso e va perciò eseguito.

Trevor Wye, 1994

La seguente storia fu trovata nel diario di appunti[3] di Moyse e deve senz'altro essere l'interpretazione conosciuta da Moyse e da altri flautisti della fiaba mitologica:

'Syrinx, devi sapere, era anticamente non uno strumento, ma una magnifica fanciulla con una voce melodiosa. Ella dava da mangiare alle sue capre, giocava con le ninfe, e cantava come fa ora [sic]. Mentre spendeva il suo tempo pascolando, giocando e cantando, Pan le si avvicinò e cercò di persuaderla a cedere ai suoi desideri, promettendole che tutte le sue capre avrebbero partorito dei gemelli. La ragazza si fece burla del suo aspetto, dicendo che non avrebbe mai accettato un amante che non fosse nè capra, nè interamente umano. Pan si getto dietro a lei per prenderla con la forza e Syrinx fuggì da Pan e dalla sua violenza. Sentendosi stanca durante il suo volo, si nascose tra alcune canne e così scomparì in una palude. Nella sua furia Pan squarciò le canne e quando non potè trovare la ragazza e capì cosa era accaduto, creò il suo strumento. Le canne che unì con della cera, erano ineguali perchè il loro amore era stato ineguale. E così lei che era una volta una magnifica ragazza è ora uno strumento musicale'.

1) Un facsimile dell'autografo con le note e parte del testo della commedia, è pubblicato da Autographus Musiscus, Malmoe, Svezia, con una introduzione di Anders Ljungar-Chapelon.
2) Vedi 'The Story of Syrinx', p.67 in *Marcel Moyse, An Extraordinary Man*. Trevor Wye, Winzer Press, U.S.A. 1993.
3) Ora in possesso dell'editore. Il brano è in inglese nell'originale.

Psyché, Atto III, Scena prima

Grotta di Pan. Attraverso l'entrata si può vedere una radura nella foresta. Un ruscello si butta in un piccolo lago. Bianche rocce sullo sfondo. Nella luce lunare, le ninfe in bianco stanno danzando, altre ninfe colgono fiori e giacciono sul bordo dell'acqua. Ogni tanto tutte si fermano e ascoltano con meraviglia il syrinx dell'invisibile Pan.

L'Oréade: Ascolta Pan che ricomincia a suonare il suo flauto.
La Naïade: È come se la notte avesse slacciato la sua cintura e lasciato cadere sulla terra silenziosa le stelle che brillano melodiosamente. Come sarebbe possibile pensare che l'amante di Euridice potesse fare dei suoni altrettanto sublimi e commuoventi sulla sua lira?
L'Oréade: Stai in silenzio, contieni la tua gioia, ascolta.